DARK
OF THE
MOON

Sara Teasdale

Dark of the Moon
Sara Teasdale

First published in 1926

This paperback edition
Published 2016

ISBN: 978-1907119354

Publisher: Tigmor Books
www.tigmorbooks.co.uk

Contents

I There Will Be Stars

On the Sussex Downs

Over the downs there were birds flying,
Far off glittered the sea,
And toward the north the weald of Sussex
Lay like a kingdom under me.

I was happier than the larks
That nest on the downs and sing to the sky,
Over the downs the birds flying
Were not so happy as I.

It was not you, though you were near,
Though you were good to hear and see,
It was not earth, it was not heaven
It was myself that sang in me.

August Night

On a midsummer night, on a night that was eerie
    with stars,
In a wood too deep for a single star to look
    through,
You led down a path whose turnings you knew in
    the darkness,
But the scent of the dew-dripping cedars was all
    that I knew.

I drank of the darkness, I was fed with the honey
    of fragrance,
I was glad of my life, the drawing of breath was
    sweet;
I heard your voice, you said. "Look down, see the
    glow-worm!"
It was there before me, a small star white at my
    feet.

We watched while it brightened as though it were
    breathed on and burning,
This tiny creature moving over earth's floor—
"L'amor che move il sole e l'altre stelle",
You said, and no more.

Two Minds

Your mind and mine are such great lovers they
Have freed themselves from cautious human clay,
And on wild clouds of thought, naked together
The ride above is in extreme delight;
We see them, we look up with a lone envy
And watch them in their zone of crystal weather
That changes not for winter or the night.

Words For An Old Air

Your heart is bound tightly, let
Beauty beware,
It is not hers to set
Free from the snare.

Tell her a bleeding hand
Bound it and tied it,
Tell her the knot will stand
Though she deride it;

One who withheld so long
All that you yearned to take,
Has made a snare too strong
For Beauty's self to break.

Mountain Water

You have taken a drink from a wild fountain
Early in the year;
There is nowhere to go from the top of a
    mountain
But down, my dear;
And the springs that flow on the floor of the
    valley
Will never seem fresh or clear
For thinking of the glitter of the mountain water
In the feathery green of the year.

At Tintagil

Iseult, Iseult, by the long waterways
Watching the wintry moon, white as a flower,
I have remembered how once in Tintagil
You heard the tread of Time hour after hour.

By casements hung with night, while all your
   women slept
You turned toward Brittany, awake ,alone,
In the high chamber hushed, save where the
   candle dripped
With the slow patient sound of blood on stone.

The ache of empty arms was an old tale to you,
And all the tragic tunes that love can play,
Yet with no woman born would you have
   changed your lot,
Though there were greater queens who had been
   gay.

There Will Be Stars

There will be stars over the place forever;
Though the house we loved and the street we
    loved are lost
Every time the earth circles her orbit
On the night the autumn equinox is crossed,
Two stars we knew, poised on the peak of
    midnight
Will reach their zenith; stillness will be deep;
There will be stars over the place forever,
There will be stars forever, while we sleep.

II Pictures Of Autumn

Autumn

(Parc Monceau)

I shall remember only these leaves falling
Small and incessant in the still air,
Yellow leaves on the dark green water resting
And the marble Venus there—
Is she pointing to her breasts or trying to hide
them?
There is no god to care.

The colonnade curves close to the leaf-strewn
water
And its reflection seems
Lost in the mass of leaves and unavailing
As a dream lost among dreams;
The colonnade curves close to the leaf-strewn
water
A dream lost among dreams.

September Day

(Pont de Neuilly)

The Seine flows out of the mist
And into the mist again;
The trees lean over the water,
The small leaves fall like rain.

The leaves fall patiently,
Nothing remembers or grieves;
The river takes to the sea
The yellow drift of the leaves.

Milky and cold is the air,
The leaves float with the stream,
The river comes out of a sleep
And goes away in a dream.

Fontainbleau

Interminable palaces front on the green parterres,
And ghosts of ladies lovely and immoral
Glide down the gilded stairs,
The high cold corridors are clicking with the heel
    taps
That long ago were theirs.

But in the sunshine, in the vague autumn
    sunshine,
The geometric gardens are desolate gay;
The crimson and scarlet and rose-red dahlias
Are painted like the ladies who used to pass this
    way
With a ringletted monarch, a Henry or a Louis
On a lost October day.

The aisles of the garden lead into the forest,
The aisles lead into autumn, a damp wind grieves,
Ghostly kings are hunting, the boar breaks cover,
But the sounds of horse and horn are hushed in
falling leaves,
Four centuries of autumns, four centuries of
    leaves.

Late October

(Bois de Boulogne)

Listen, the damp leaves on the walks are blowing
With a ghost of sound;
Is it a fog or is it a rain dripping
From the low trees to the ground?

If I had gone before, I could have remembered
Lilacs and green afternoons of May;
I chose to wait, I chose to hear from autumn
Whatever she has to say.

III Sand Drift

"Beautiful Proud Sea"

Careless forever, beautiful proud sea,
You laugh in happy thunder all alone,
You fold upon yourself, you dance your dance
Impartially on drift-weed, sand or stone.

You make us believe that we can outlive death,
You make us for an instant, for your sake,
Burn, like stretched silver of a wave,
Not breaking, but about o break.

Land's End

The shores of the world are ours, the solitary
Beaches that bear no fruit, nor any flowers,
Only the harsh sea-grass that the wind harries
Hours on unbroken hours.

No one will envy us these empty reaches
At the world's end, and none will care that we
Leave our lost footprints where the sand forever
Takes the unchanging passion of the sea.

Sand Drift

I thought I should not walk these dunes again,
Nor feel the sting of this wind-bitten sand
Where the coarse grasses always blow one way,
Bent, as my thoughts are, by an unseen hand.

I have returned; where the last wave rushed up
The wet sand is a mirror for the sky
A bright blue instant, and along its sheen
the nimble sandpipers run twinkling by.
Nothing has changed; with the same hollow
    thunder
The waves die in their everlasting snow—
Only the place we sat is drifted over,
Lost in the blowing sand, long, long ago.

Blue Stargrass

If we took the old path
In the old field
The same gate would stand there
That will never yield.

Where the sun warmed us
With a cloak made of gold,
The rain would be falling
And the wind would be cold;

And we would stop to search
In the wind and he rain,
But we would not find the stargrass
By the path again.

September Night

We walked in the dew, in the drowsy starlight
To the sleepless, sleepy sound
Of insects singing in the low sea-meadows
For miles and miles around;
With a wheel and a whirr the resistless rhythm
Trembled incessantly;
Antares was red in the sky before us,
And behind us, the blackness of the sea.

Low Tide

The birds are gathering over the dunes,
Swerving and wheeling in shifting flight,
A thousand wings sweep darkly by
Over the dunes and out of sight.

Why did you bring me down to the sea
With the gathering birds and the fish-hawk flying,
The tide is low and the wind is hard,
Nothing is left but the old year dying.

I wish I were one of the gathering birds,
Two sharp black wings would be good for me—
When noting is left but the old year dying,
Why did you bring me down to the sea?

IV Portraits

Effigy of a Nun (Sixteenth Century)

Infinite gentleness, infinite irony
Are in this face with fast-sealed eyes,
And round this mouth that learned in loneliness
How useless their wisdom is to the wise.

In her nun's habit carved, patiently, lovingly,
By one who knew the ways of womankind,
This woman's face still keeps, in its cold wistful
    calm,
All of the subtle pride of her mind.

These long patrician hands, clasping the crucifix,
Show she has weighed the world, her will was set;
These pale curved lips of hers, holding their
    hidden smile,
Once having made their choice, knew no regret.

She was of those who hoard their own thoughts
    carefully,
Feeling them far too dear to give away,
Content to look at life with the high, insolent
Air of an audience watching a play.

If she was curious, if she was passionate
She must have told herself that love was great,
But that the lacking it might be as great a thing
If she held fast to it, challenging fate.

She who so loved herself and her warring
    thoughts,
Watching their humorous, tragic rebound,
In her thick habit's fold, sleeping, sleeping,
Is she amused at dreams she has found?

Infinite tenderness, infinite irony
Are hidden forever in her closed eyes,
Who must have learned too well in her long
    loneliness
How empty wisdom is, even to the wise.

Those Who Love

Those who love the most,
Do not talk of their love,
Francesca, Guinevere,
Deirdre, Iseult, Heloise,
In the fragrant gardens of heaven
Are silent, or speak if at all
Of fragile, inconsequential things.

And a woman I used to know
Who loved one man from her youth,
Against the strength of the fates
Fighting in somber pride,
Never spoke of this thing,
But hearing his name by chance,
Alight would pass over her face.

Epitaph

Serene descent, as a red leaf's descending
When there is neither wind nor noise of rain,
But only autumn air and the unending
Drawing of all things to the earth again:

So be it; let the snow sift deep and cover
All that was drunken once with light and air;
The earth will not regret her tireless lover,
Nor he awake to know she does not care.

Appraisal

Never think she loves him wholly,
Never believe her love is blind,
All his faults are locked securely
In a closet of her mind;
All his indecisions folded
Like old flags that time has faded,
Limp and streaked with rain.
And his cautiousness like garments
Frayed and thin, with many a stain—
Let them be, oh let them be,
There is treasure to outweigh them,
His proud will that sharply stirred,
Climbs as surely as the tide,
Senses strained too taut to sleep,
Gentleness to beast and bird,
Humour flickering hushed and wide
As the moon on moving water,
And a tenderness too deep
To be gathered in a word.

The Wise Woman

She must be rich who can forego
An hour so jewelled with delight,
She must have treasuries of joy
That she can draw on day and night,
She must be very sure of heaven—
Or is it only that she feels
How much more safe it is to lack
A thing that time so often steals

She Who Could Bind You

She who could bind you
Could bind fire to a wall;
She who could hold you
Could hold a waterfall;
She who could keep you
Could keep the wind from blowing
On a warm spring night
With a low moon glowing.

"So This Was All"

So this was all there was to the great play
She came so far to act in, this was all—
Except the short last scene and the slow fall
Of the final curtain, that might catch half-way,
As final curtains do, and leave the grey
Lorn end of things to long exposed. the hall
Clapped faintly, and she took her curtain call,
Knowing how little she had left to say.
And in the pause before the last act started,
Slowly unpinning the roses she had worn,
She reconsidered lines that had been said,
And found them hardly worthy the high-hearted
Ardor that she had brought, nor the bright, torn,
Roses that shattered round her, dripping red.

V Midsummer Nights

Twilight

(Nahant)

There was an evening when the sky was clear,
Ineffably translucent in its blue;
The tide was falling and the sea withdrew
In hushed and happy music from the sheer
Shadowy granite of the cliffs; and fear
Of what life may be, and what death can do,
Fell from us like steel armor, and we knew
The wisdom of the Law that holds us here.
It was a though we saw the Secret Will
It was as though we floated and were free;
In the south-west a planet shone serenely,
And the high moon, most reticent and queenly,
Seeing the earth has darkened and grown still,
Misted with light the meadows of the sea.

Full Moon

(Santa Barbara)

I listened, there was not a sound to hear
In the great rain of moonlight pouring down,
The eucalyptus trees were carved in silver
And a light mist of silver lulled the town.

I saw far off the grey Pacific bearing
A broad white disk of flame,
And on the garden walk a snail beside me
Tracing in crystal the slow way he came.

The Fountain

Fountain, fountain, what do you say
Singing at night alone?
"It is enough to rise and fall
Here in my basin of stone."

But are you content as you seem to be
So near the freedom and rush of the sea?
"I have listened all night to its labouring sound,
It haves and sags, as the moon runs round;
Ocean and fountain, shadow and tree,
Nothing escapes, nothing is free."

Clear Evening

The crescent moon is large enough to linger
A little while after the twilight goes,
This moist midsummer night the garden perfumes
Are earth and apple, dewy pine and rose.

Over my head four new-cut stars are glinting
And the inevitable night draws on;
I am alone, the old terror takes me,
Evenings will come like this when I am gone;

Evenings on evenings, years on years forever—
Be taut, my spirit, close upon and keep
The scent, the brooding chill, the gliding fire-fly,
A poem learned before I fall asleep.

Not by the Sea

Not by the sea, but somewhere in the hills,
Not by the sea, but in the uplands surely
There must be rest where a dim pool demurely
Watches all night the stern slow-moving skies;

Not by the sea, that never was appeased,
Not by the sea, whose immemorial longing
Shames the tired earth where even longing dies,
Not by the sea that bore Iseult and Helen,
But in a dark green hollow of the hills
There must be sleep, even for the sleepless eyes.

Midsummer Night

Midsummer night without a moon, but the stars
In a serene bright multitude were there,
Even the shyest ones, even the faint motes shining
Low in the north, under the Little Bear.

When I have said, "This tragic farce I play in
Has neither dignity, delight nor end,"
The holy night draws all its stars around me,
I am ashamed, I have betrayed my Friend.

VI The Crystal Gazer

The Crystal Gazer

I shall gather myself into myself again,
I shall take my scattered selves and make them
    one,
Fusing them into a polished crystal ball
Where I can see the moon and the flashing sun.

I shall sit like a sibyl, hour after hour intent,
Watching the future come and the present go,
And the little shifting pictures of people rushing
In restless self-importance to and fro.

The Solitary

My heart has grown rich with the passing of
     years,
I have less need now than when I was young
To share myself with every comer
Or shape my thoughts into words with my tongue

It is one to me that they come or go
If I have myself and the drive of my will,
And strength to climb on a summer night
And watch the stars swarm over the hill.

Let them think I love them more than I do,
Let them think I care, though I go alone;
If it lifts their pride, what is it to me
Who am self-complete as a flower or a stone.

Day's Ending

(Tucson)

Aloof as aged kings,
Wearing like them the purple,
The mountains ring the mesa
crowned with a dusky light;
Many a time I watched
That coming-on of darkness
Till stars burned through the heavens
Intolerably bright.

It was not long I lived there
But I became a woman
Under those vehement stars,
For it was there I heard
For the first tie my spirit
Forging an iron rule for me,
As though with slow cold hammers
Beating out word by word:

"Only yourself can heal you,
Only yourself can lead you,
The road is heavy going
And ends where no man knows;
Take love when love is given,
But never think to find it
A sure escape from sorrow
or a complete repose."

A Reply

Four people knew the very me,
Four is enough, so let it be;
For the rest I make no chart,
There are no highroads to my heart;
The gates are locked, they will not stir
For any ardent traveller.
I have not been misunderstood,
And on the whole, I think life good—
So waste no sympathy on me
Or any well-meant gallantry;
I have enough to do to muse
On memories I would not lose.

Leisure

If I should make no poems any more
There would be rest at least, so let it be;
Time to read books in other tongues and listen
To the long mellow thunder of the sea.

The year will turn for me, I shall delight in
All animals, and some of my own kind,
Sharing with no one but myself the frosty
And half ironic musings of my mind.

I Shall Live to be Old

I shall live to be old, who feared I should die
    young,
I shall live to be old,
I shall cling to life as the leaves to the creaking
    oak
In the rustle of falling snow and the cold.

The other trees let loose their leaves on the air
In their russet and red,
I have lived long enough to wonder which is the
    best,
And to envy sometimes the way of the early dead.

Wisdom

It was a night of early spring,
The winter-sleep was scarcely broken;
Around us shadows and the wind
Listened for what was never spoken.

Though half a score of years are gone,
Spring comes as sharply mow as then—
But if we had it all to do
It would be done the same again.

It was a spring that never came,
But we have lived enough to know
What we have never had, remains;
It is the things we have that go.

The Old Enemy

Rebellion against death, the old rebellion
Is over; I have nothing left to fight;
Battles have always had their need of music
But peace is quiet as a windless night.

Therefore I make no songs—I have grown certain
Save when he comes too late, death is a friend,
A shepherd leading home his flock serenely
Under the planet at the evening's end.

VII Berkshire Notes

Winter Sun

(Lenox)

There was a bush with scarlet berries
And there hemlocks heaped with snow;
With a sound like surf on long sea-beaches
they took the wind and let it go.

The hills were shining in their samite,
Fold after fold they flowed away—
"Let come what may," your eyes were saying,
"At least we two have had to-day."

A December Day

Dawn turned on her purple pillow
And late, late came the winter day,
Snow was curved to the boughs of the willow,
The sunless world was white and grey.

At noon we heard a blue-jay scolding,
At five the last thin light was lost
From snow-banked windows faintly holding
The feathery filigree of frost.

February Twilight

I stood beside a hill
Smooth with new-laid snow,
A single star looked out
From the cold evening glow.

There was no other creature
That saw what I could see—
I stood and watched the evening star
As long as it watched me.

"I Have Seen the Spring"

Nothing is new, I have seen the spring too often;
There have been other plum-trees white as this
    one
Like a silvery cloud tethered beside the road,
I have been waked from sleep too many times
By birds at dawn boasting their love is beautiful.
The grass-blades gleam in the wind, nothing is
    changed.
Nothing is lost, it is all as it used to be,
Unopened lilacs are still as deep a purple,
The boughs of the elm are dancing still in a veil of
    tiny leaves,
Nothing is lost but as few years from my life.

Wind Elegy

(W. E. W.)

Only the wind knows he is gone,
Only the wind grieves,
The sun shines, the fields are sown,
Sparrows mate in the eaves;

But I heard the wind in the pines he planted
And the hemlocks overhead,
"His acres wake, for the year turns,
But he is asleep," it said.

In the Wood

I heard the waterfall rejoice
Singing like a choir,
I saw the sun flash out of it
Azure and amber fire.

The earth was like an open flower
Enamelled and arrayed,
The path I took to find its heart
Fluttered with sun and shade.

And while earth lured me, gently, gently,
Happy and all alone,
Suddenly a heavy snake reared
black upon a stone.

Autumn Dusk

I saw above a sea of hills
A solitary planet shine
And there was no one near or far
To keep the world from being mine.

VIII Arcturus In Autumn

Arcturus in Autumn

When, in the gold October dusk, I saw you near
    to setting,
Arcturus, bringer of spring,
Lord of the summer nights, leaving us now i
    autumn,
Having no pity on our withering;

Oh then I knew at last that my own autumn was
    upon me,
I felt it in my blood,
Restless as dwindling streams that still remember
The music of their flood.

There in the thickening dark a wind a wind-bent
    tree above me
Loosed its last leaves in flight—
I saw you sink and vanish, pitiless Arcturus,
You will not stay to share our lengthening night.

"I Could Snatch a Day"

I could snatch a day out of the late autumn
And set it trembling like forgotten springs,
There would be sharp blue skies with new leaves
    shining
And flying shadows cast by flying wings.

I could take the heavy wheel of the world and
    break it,
But we sit brooding while the ashes fall,
Cowering over an old fire that dwindles,
Waiting for nothing at all.

An End

I have no heart for any other joy,
The drenched September day turns to depart,
And I have said good-bye to what I love;
With my own will I vanquished my own heart.

On the long wind I hear the winter coming,
The window panes are cold and blind with rain;
With my own will I turned the summer from me
And summer will not come again.

Foreknown

They brought me with a secret glee
The news I knew before they spoke,
And though they hoped to see me riven,
They found me light as dry leaves driven
Before the storm that splits an oak.

For I had learned from many an autumn
The way a leaf can drift and go,
Lightly, lightly, almost gay
Taking the unreturning way
To mix with winter and the snow.

Winter

I shall have winter now and lessening days,
Lit by a smoky sun with slanting rays,
And after falling leaves, the first determined frost.
The colors of the world will all be lost.
So be it; the faint buzzing of the snow
Will fill the empty boughs,
And after sleet storms I shall wake to see
A glittering glassy plume of every tree.
Nothing shall tempt me from my fire-lit house,
And I shall find at night a friendly ember
And make my life of what I can remember.

Winter Night Song

Will you come as of old with singing,
And shall I hear as of old?
Shall I rush to open the window
In spite of the arrowy cold?

Ah no, my dear, ah no,
I shall sit by the fire reading,
Though you sing half the night in the snow
I shall not be heeding.

Though your voice remembers the forest,
The warm green light and the birds,
Though you gather the sea in your singing
And pour its sound into words,

Even so, my dear, even so,
I shall not heed you at all;
Though your shoulders are white with snow,
Though you strain your voice to a call,
I shall drowse and the fire will drowse,
The draught will be cold on the floor,
the clock running down,
Snow banking the door.

Never Again

Never again the music blown as brightly
Off of my heart as foam blown off a wave;
Never again the melody that lightly
Caressed my grief and healed the wounds it gave.

Never again—I hear my dark thoughts clashing
Sullen and blind as waves that beat a wall—
Age that is coming, summer that is going,
All I have lost or never found at all.

The Tune

I know a certain tune that my life plays;
Over and over I have heard it start
With all the wavering loveliness of viols
And gain in swiftness like a runner's heart.

It climbs and climbs; I watch it sway in climbing
High over time, high even over doubt,
It has all heaven to itself—it pauses
And faltering blindly down the air, goes out.

IX The Flight

The Beloved

It is enough of honour for one lifetime
To have known you better than the rest have
    known,
The shadows and the colors of your voice,
Your will, immutable and still as stone.

The shy heart, so lonely and so gay,
The sad laughter and the pride of pride,
The tenderness, the depth of tenderness
Rich as the earth, and wide as heaven is wide.

"When I Am Not With You"

When I am not with you
I am alone,
For there is no one else
And there is nothing
That comforts me but you.
When you are gone
Suddenly I am sick,
Blackness is round me,
There is nothing left.
I have tried many things,
Music and cities,
Stars in their constellations
And the sea,
But there is nothing
That comforts me but you;
And my poor pride bows down
Like grass in a rain-storm
Drenches with my longing.
The night is unbearable,
Oh let me go to you
For there is no one,
There is nothing
To comfort me but you.

Dedication

At least I have loved you;
Though much went wrong,
This was good,
This was strong.

Unshaken
In spite of the going of years,
Too sure to retract,
Too proud for tears.

Let my love be the pillow
Under your head,
On your lips like a song,
To your hunger, bread.

On a March Day

here in the teeth of this triumphant wind
That shakes the naked shadows on the ground,
Making a key-board of the earth to strike
From clattering tree and hedge a separate sound,

Bear witness for me that I loved my life,
All things that hurt me and all things that healed,
And that I swore to it this new-broken field.

You only knew me, tell them I was glad
For every hour since my hour of birth,
And that I ceased to fear, as once I feared,
the last complete reunion with the earth.

Let It Be You

Let it be you who lean above me
On my last day,
Let it be you who shut my eyelids
Forever and aye.

Say a "Good-night" as you have said it
All of these years,
With the old look, with the old whisper
And without tears.

You will know then all that in silence
You always knew,
Though I have loved, I loved no other
As I love you.

The Flight

We are two eagles
Flying together
Under the heavens,
Over the mountains,
Stretched on the wind.
Sunlight heartens us,
Blind snow baffles us,
Clouds wheel after us
Ravelled and thinned.

We are like eagles,
But when Death harries us,
Human and humbled
When one of us goes,
Let the other follow,
Let the flight be ended,
Let the fire blacken,
Let the book close.

Printed in Great Britain
by Amazon